Ashbo[illegible]es Town[illegible]l

Welcome to Ashbourne - A Georgian Market Town in the Derbyshire Dales at the edge of the Peak District

The Ashbourne area has been occupied for many thousands of years. Recorded history starts in 1086 with an entry in the Doomsday Book as Esseburne. The town acquired borough status around 1190 and continued to expand but seems to have been largely rebuilt to a predetermined plan after a disastrous fire in 1252.

This location, where the hills meet the dales and drovers roads crossed a salt-way developed into a major trading centre for the area from the 1730s onwards and Ashbourne became an important stop on the main London to Carlisle road and large coaching Inns became established.

The Georgian period was the high point in Ashbourne's development with many of the local gentry building or rebuilding town houses and a prosperous middle class expanding to meet their needs and those of the increasing number of visitors to the area. The need to accommodate additional workers and their families saw many of the 'Yards' developed behind the fine houses as the burgage plots were built over or developed for commercial purposes.

The coming of the railways in early Victorian times brought this prosperity to an end as road transport declined and Ashbourne lost its importance as a cross roads. Today in Church Street we have one of the finest Georgian streets in Derbyshire with some 10 major period houses, an Elizabethan school building, medieval church and Tudor almshouses. In the marketplace the mainly Victorian shopfronts hide ancient timber frame buildings and the many Yards contain hidden gems just off the main streets.

Alan Cockayne

This guide has been produced by the Ashbourne Treasures Group who wish to acknowledge and thank for their kind help and support - The Heritage Lottery Fund, The Old Trust, Queen Elizabeth's Grammar School, Ashbourne Heritage Society, The Old Ashburnians, The Ashbourne Partnership, Derbyshire Dales District Council, Derbyshire County Council and especially, Geof Cole for the written content, Sue Prince for the trail map and John Dawson for the period photographs.

Cover: 1547 Map of Ashbourne - courtesy of The National Archives at Kew.

The walk can start at any of the three original Ashbourne Treasures exhibition centres: See the map at the end of the book for key sites and locations.

The Ashbourne Library in Compton. (1)

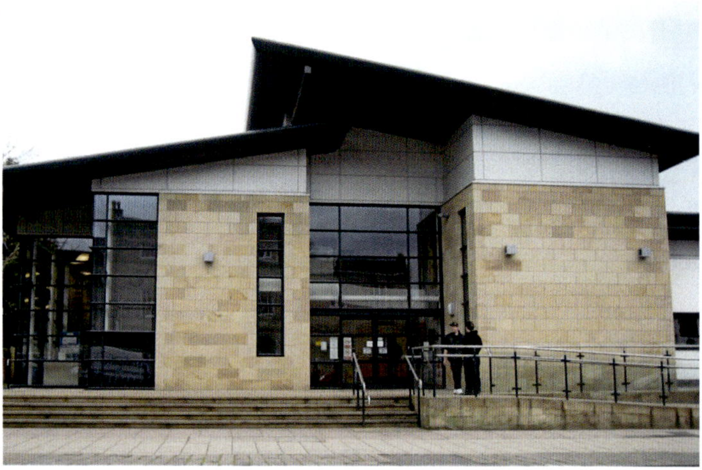

The Heritage Centre at 13 Church Street. (10)

St Oswald's Church. Church Street. (7)

When walking around the town don't forget to look at the upper floors and rooflines which can tell you a lot about the history of the building. It is a circular route that takes about one and a half hours to complete, allowing time to look at the locations featured. If time permits there are two possible extensions:

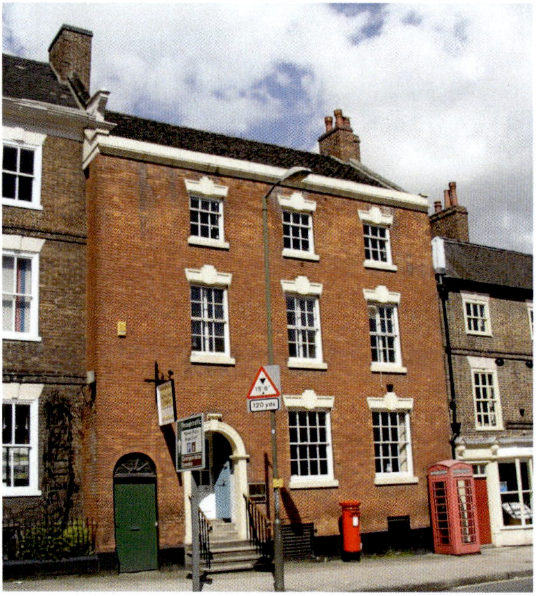

Extension 1: to ***St John's Church*** on Buxton Hill, which starts at the top of the Market Place.

Extension 2: *Ashbourne Hall and Town Park,* which starts at Shawcroft car park.

For more information on the history and heritage of the buildings. places, people and events in Ashbourne please see the Ashbourne Treasures book or go online and visit the 'Our Ashbourne' website at http://ourashbourne.co.uk or visit The Ashbourne Heritage Centre in Church Street, opening days and times may vary throughout the year.

Ashbourne Library is at the top of a street called ***Compton***, which was also originally the name of the area and was not part of Ashbourne until 1873. The name Compton may go back to before the Norman Conquest. The existence of a market in Campdene Street (modern Compton) is mentioned in a document of 1274, and may mean "the valley where a fight occurred".

Between 875 and 925, Ashbourne was on the border of the areas controlled by the English and the Danes, and so a skirmish around Compton is quite possible. (1)

Cross the street carefully to Compton House (now Lloyds Bank)

Compton House was built in the 1760s for Francis Beresford, an attorney who had made a fortune from coal mining and the Butterley Company at Ripley. The house was designed by the Derby architect Joseph Pickford.

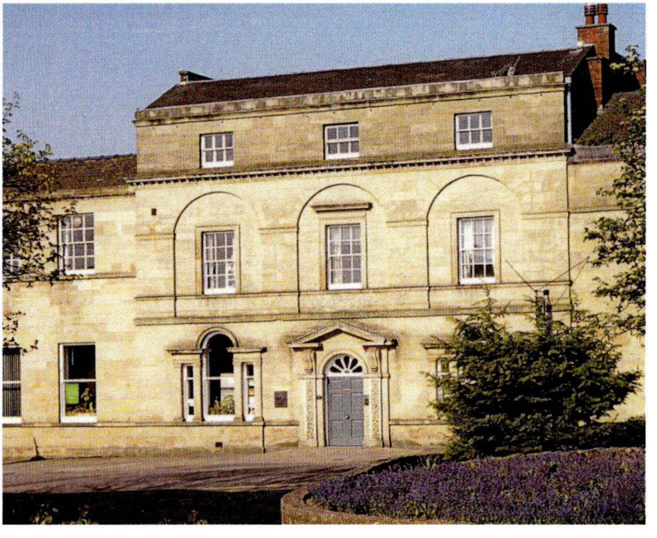

The facade is in stone, but the sides and back are brick. It is surprising that the house butts onto the road rather than being set back and was built in the poorer part of Ashbourne.

Cross the bridge into Dig Street

The old stone bridge crosses the ***Henmore***. This brook was called Scolebrook as early as 1226, but by the time Charles Cotton published Part 2 of *The Compleat Angler* in 1676, it was known as the Henmore. The brook is the traditional boundary between the two Shrovetide Football teams. People born or connected with the Ashbourne side of the brook are Up'ards, whilst those born or connected with the Compton side are Down'ards. (2)

Look over the bridge parapet. At the rear of the building on your right, you will see a lower level window. This was once part of the town's workhouse and quite often flooded.

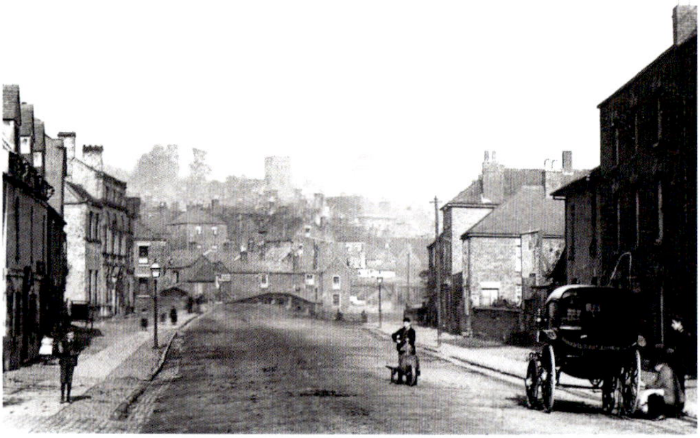

The building immediately after the bridge, now the ***Bridge Restaurant***, was once the ***Three Horse Shoes*** public house. It was converted into a cycle shop and later, Foster Brothers fishing tackle shop. This shop closed in 2000, but its cane rods are still highly valued and are collected by enthusiasts. The yard alongside of the restaurant was ***Work House Yard***, which had some of the worst overcrowded slums in the town. It contained mostly lodgings for labourers; in the 1851 census, one house in the yard was recorded as having fifteen people living there, thirteen of them Irish labourers. Conditions were poor and as late as 1893 eight people died here from a typhoid outbreak. The yard was finally cleared in the early 20th century.

Continue to walk up Dig Street to The Cheddar Gorge

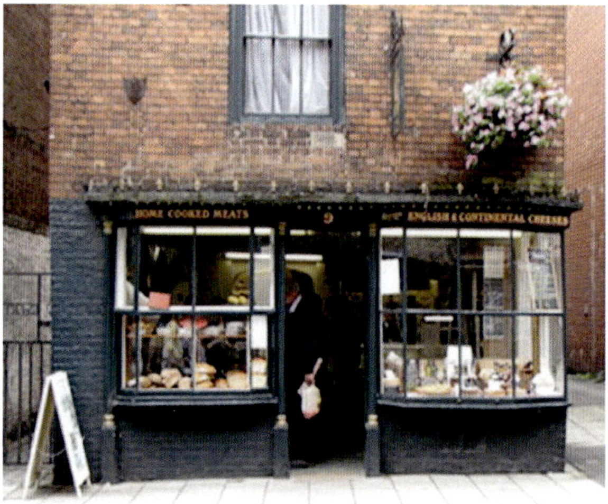

Dig Street appears to be a corruption of Ditch Street. It is possibly on the line of a shallow rivulet connecting into the Henmore and may have acted as a drain from the Market Place into the brook. Nearly every property on Dig Street has a shop frontage making it primarily a commercial street.

The Cheddar Gorge, 9 Dig Street, was probably built in the late 18th century. However, the shop front is most likely 19th century and is a rare example in Ashbourne of a shop front from that period.

Continue along the street to The Corner House at the road junction

The Corner House (with its square-faced clock using letters instead of numbers) is a plain late Georgian or Regency commercial building with a modern shop front (now ***Avanti Jewellers***). In 1822, Arkwright, Toplis and Co, who already had a bank in Wirksworth, converted the whole building into a bank. The son of the inventor and entrepreneur Richard Arkwright, Richard Arkwright Junior's interests lay mainly in banking, investment in government funds and the accumulation of land. In 1804 he became a partner in the Toplis Bank at Wirksworth and in 1829 after the death of John Toplis, he took complete control. It was a small but highly profitable business, serving local gentry and industry. He lived for a time at Ashbourne Hall. He also lent money to the nobility, most famously to Georgiana, Duchess of Devonshire, for her gambling debts, which stood at £60,000 when she died. Richard Arkwright Junior was believed to be the richest commoner in Britain when he died in 1843.

Turn left and walk along Church Street

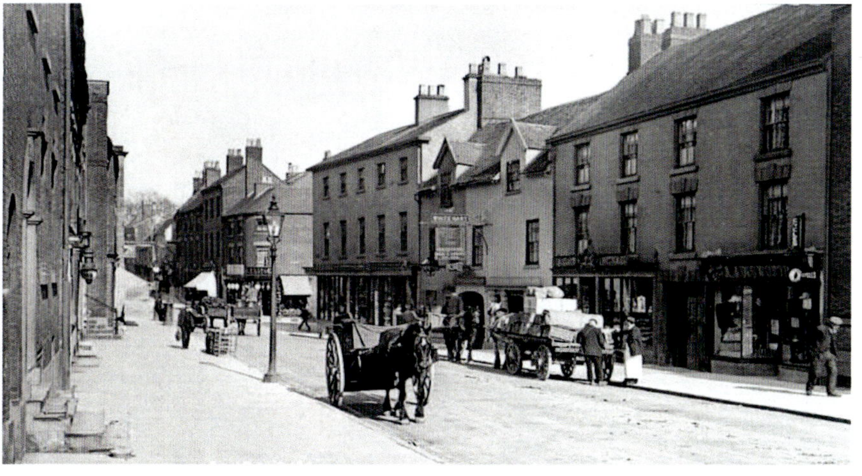

This street was described by architectural historian Nikolas Pevsner as "*one of the finest streets in Derbyshire*". The ***White Hart*** was one of Ashbourne's coaching inns with stabling for horses and a malthouse in the narrow yard. It was also the site of a cockpit, where cockfighting was held; local gentry, who owned fighting cocks, would gamble, often large amounts, on the outcome. (3)

Continue along Church Street to the ***Clergy Widows Almshouses,*** a block of four houses grouped around a courtyard. Note the very high quality brickwork needing only a thin layer of mortar between brick courses. To achieve this required very consistent high quality bricks, not easy or cheap at a time when bricks were handmade. It was built under the 1710 will of an Ashbourne-born London businessman, Nicholaus Spalden for *"the widows of 4 clergymen of the Church of England*". A legal dispute over his will in the Courts of Chancery delayed their building for over fifty years. It is now six flats. (4)

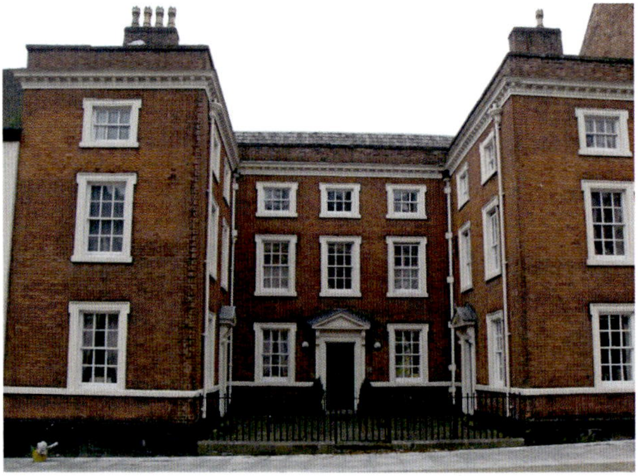

The house next door, now ***Hulme's Fish Shop,*** was built about 1710. It is unusual having the front divided into three bays by giant fluted pilasters (decorative features that project from the wall in the shape of a column). The shop front was added in the 1930s, when Albert Hulme converted the house into a fish, game and poultry shop, which is still in business today. At the back, a late 18th century former malthouse survives. There is a small coach house before the next property, ***No. 28 Church Street***, now a series of antique shops. This was one of the major gentleman's residences in Ashbourne, built about 1720. It has seven uniform bays, a brick parapet, and a fine 'shell' canopy over the central door.

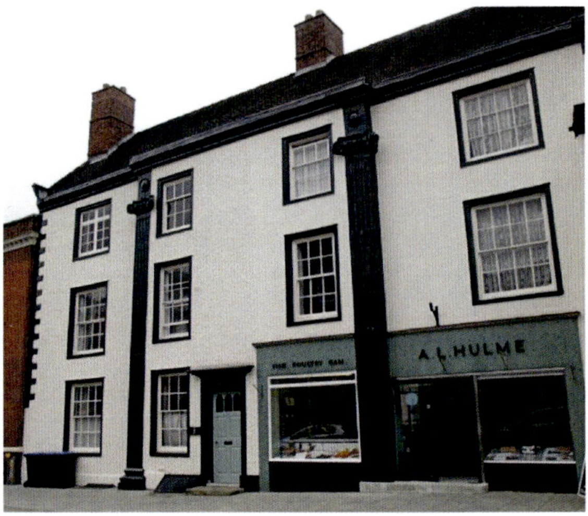

Continue along to the Methodist Chapel

The Methodist Chapel was erected between 1879 and 1881 to replace an earlier Wesleyan Chapel in Compton. The new chapel has a distinctive Renaissance-style front decorated with terracotta panels and friezes. It was the work of the architect John Wills, whose Derby practice specialised in non-conformist chapels and produced lavish designs where money was available.

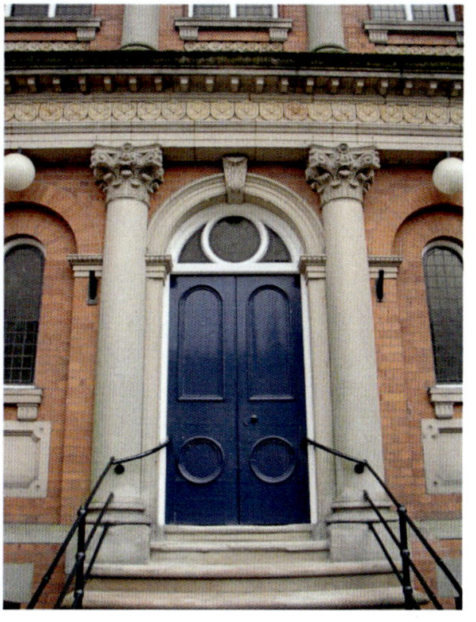

It was intended to look very different from the 'Gothic' Anglican churches. However, not everyone appreciated the design: the architectural historian Nikolaus Pevsner described the chapel as a "pretentious eyesore". (5)

When the railway was extended from Ashbourne to Buxton in 1899, some Georgian properties next to the chapel were demolished to make way for the line and Ashbourne's first new road since medieval times, ***Station Road,*** was created.

At this time, the Methodist Chapel was extended to provide some lock-up shops (now the ***Cornerstone Café***) and a church hall (***Century Hall***). Look at the interesting Arts and Crafts decorative features on both buildings. The complex was used as an auxiliary hospital in WW1.

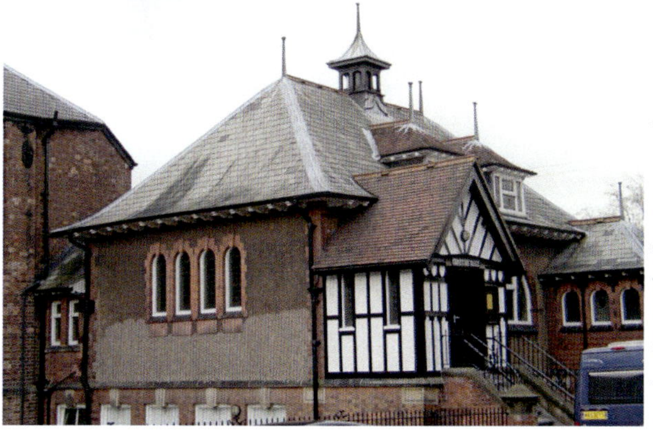

Cross Station Road

Cross Station Road carefully and examine the front of the next two houses ***No. 38 Church Street*** was a three-storey building but, with the raising of the road to accommodate the railway, the lower two stories were effectively amalgamated into one.

Hulland House next door was another major gentleman's house built about 1740, but with an additional western wing with arched carriageway entry added in 1790. It was the home of the Walker family, who made a fortune from tanning leather. The ground floor is partly obscured by the raised street level.

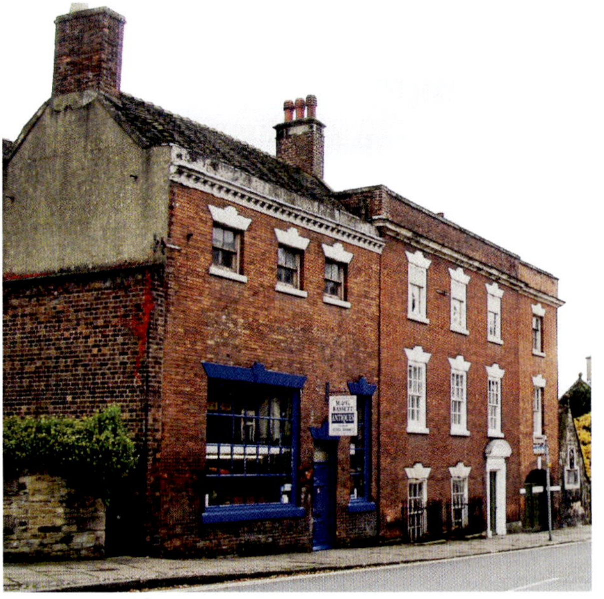

Continue to the alms houses and on to The Mansion

The first group are ***Pegge's Almshouses*** built at right angles to the street around 1699. The Pegge family coat of arms, a chevron between three pegs, is on the end of the building. The crest is a 'rebus' – a puzzle that uses pictures to represent words. The Cokayne family crest with three cockerels (adopted by both the town and the Grammar School) is another. Pegge's Almshouses are now in private ownership with one a holiday let. The second group, parallel to the street is ***Owfield's Almshouses***, which are still in use as almshouses. They were built between 1615 and 1625, with a second storey added in 1848. In a trade directory of 1822, they are described as *"for aged and broken down house-keepers"*. They were restored in 1990, when two were turned into one.

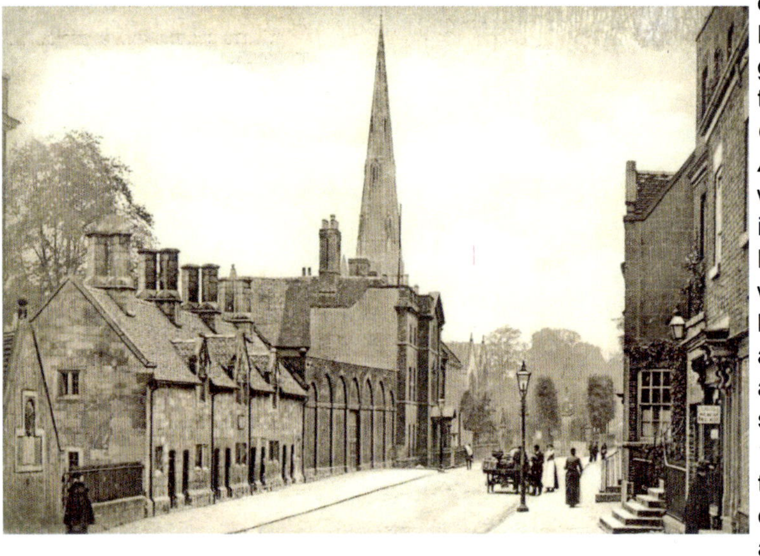

The Mansion is the largest and most imposing gentleman's house in Ashbourne and probably its oldest surviving brick building. Originally built in the 1680s, possibly around an earlier timber framed building, it was re-built in the 1760s to the latest fashion, possibly in answer to the work done on The Grey House opposite, albeit in brick rather than stone. Joseph Pickford of Derby, whose house in Friargate, Derby, is now a museum, and who also worked for Josiah Wedgwood in Stoke and the Fitz-Herberts at Tissington, probably carried out the work on both houses. The Mansion had a large paddock where Dr John Taylor, the owner, bred Highland cattle. Dr Samuel Johnson, famous for writing the first English dictionary, was an old school friend of Dr Taylor and visited him here. Above the door is a Latin verse by Johnson which translates as *"May this house stand until the tortoise walks around the world and until the ant drains the ocean waves".* (6)

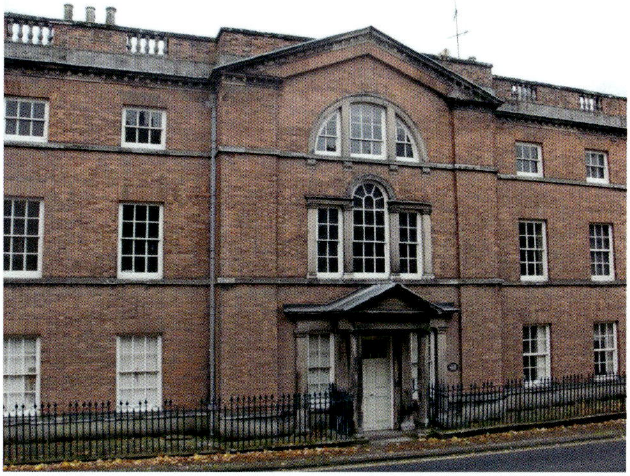

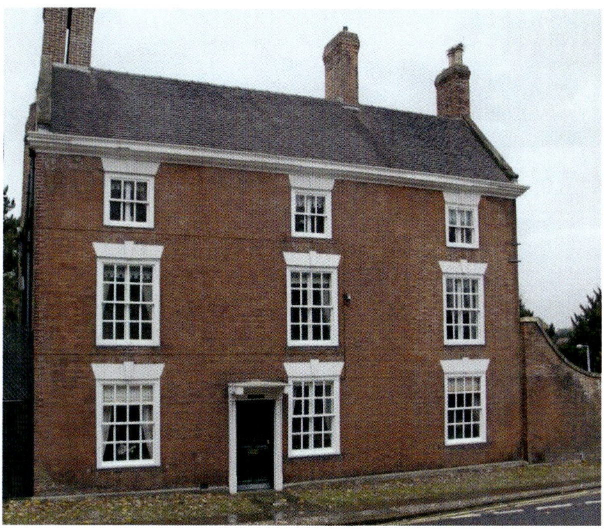

The last house in Church Street, ***The Old House,*** had a late Georgian frontage added onto a late 17th or early 18th century house, which probably explains the unbalanced proportions and off-centre doorway. It is best known as the home of the Hollick family; the father and son were well respected local doctors. In his spare time, Dr Hollick and his daughter Kathleen planted daffodils in the churchyard.

Cross School Lane to the churchyard and St Oswald's Church

The **church gates** date from the early 1700s and are probably by the respected Derbyshire ironsmith Robert Bakewell; note the skulls and flames on the top of the pillars, possibly intended to remind people of their mortality and impending judgment.

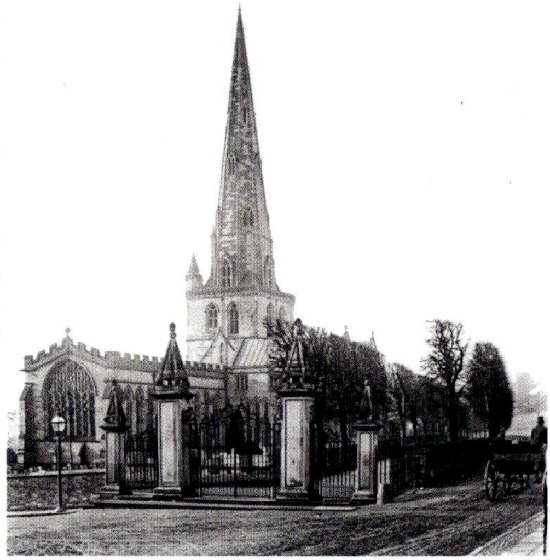

When John Ruskin visited in 1875, he was not impressed with the skulls and suggested that the town "*applied the funds it had at its disposal to give honest labourers work to break up the skull obelisks for road metal*".

Fortunately, his advice was not followed, but we still have potholes in the roads!

The Victorian writer George Eliot described ***St Oswald's Church*** as *"the finest mere parish church in the Kingdom"*. It has a **slender spire 212 feet (65m) high** and was once a candidate to be the cathedral for the Derby Diocese. A church at Ashbourne is mentioned in the Domesday Book of 1086, though this was almost certainly a wooden building. The existing church dates from the early 1200s and the 1241 dedication plaque (in St Oswald's Chapel in the South Transept) is believed to be the oldest in the country. (7)

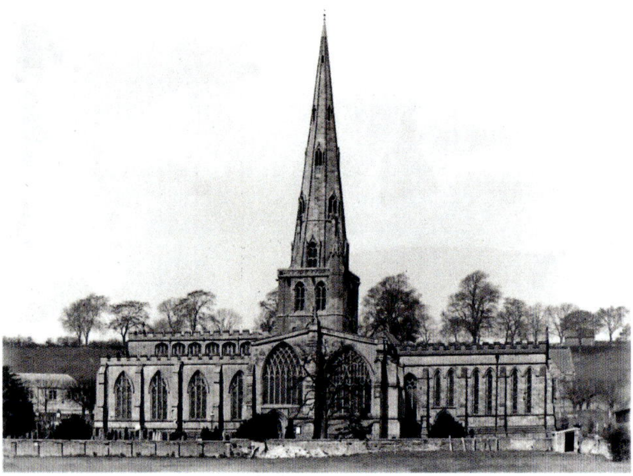

The oldest parts of the current building are the chancel (eastern end of the church containing the altar) and the transepts (the arms of the church). The main part of the nave (the body of the church where the congregation sits) was added in the mid-13th century and widened later in the century when a tower was also added. The last major construction was the spire built early in the 14th century.

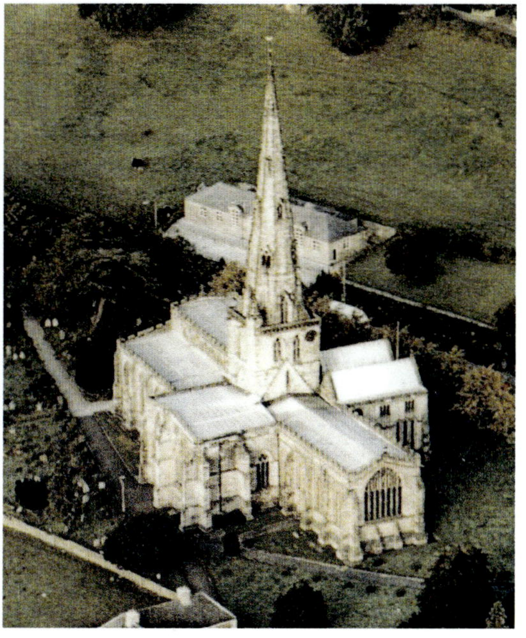

A north aisle was never built, possibly because of the impact of the Black Death from 1348, but the **east window** (the one facing the entrance gates) is the earliest perpendicular style window in Derbyshire, dated by the crests in the glass to between 1392 and 1399.

George Gilbert Scott, of Albert Memorial fame, worked on the chancel and introduced the castellations on the chancel roof in the 1870s, possibly to match those on the nave.

Legend says that a spring under the tower, found during strengthening work in the early 1900s, was the site of pagan worship. Inside the church are some interesting monuments and excellent stained glass, ranging from medieval to Arts and Crafts. The settlement mentioned in the Domesday Book of 1086 would have been located around the church, before the new town was developed in the middle of the 13th century.

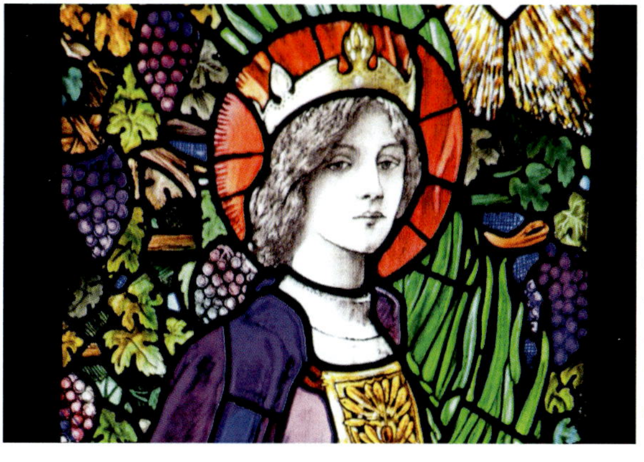

Return to the Church Gates and cross the road carefully

Immediately opposite the church gates is ***Hanson Mount***, a restored 17th century building. During the late 1700s, the house was divided into three to house separate families, but is now a single home once again.

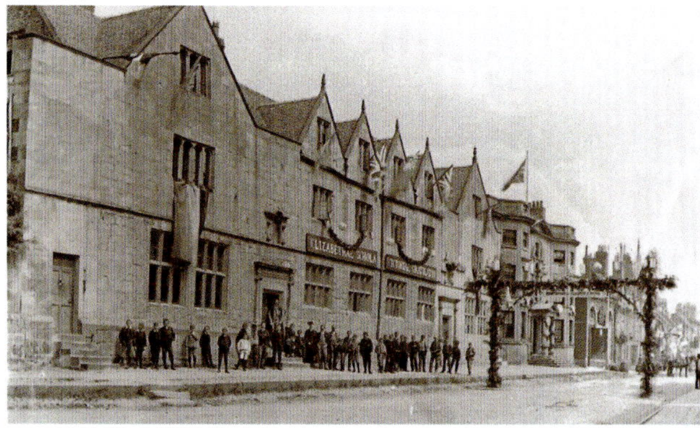

Start to head back into town. The next building is ***The Old Grammar School,*** an Elizabethan building that was comprised of a central ground-floor schoolroom with dormitories above, flanked on either side by houses for the headmaster and undermaster. Five townsfolk petitioned Queen Elizabeth I for a school on the grounds that *"for lack of education, the inhabitants were given over to wickedness and vices such as idleness, swearing, drunkenness, whoredom and the like".* The Queen issued a foundation charter in 1585, but work was not completed until 1603. Only boys were admitted, aged between six and nine; they had to be able to read and write and were assessed for their religious knowledge and morality. In 1909, a new school (the present Queen Elizabeth's Grammar School - QEGS) was opened at the other end of the town, and girls were admitted for the first time. For a time, the Old School was used a dormitory for boys who boarded at QEGS, whilst girls lived with the headmaster's family in the Mansion opposite. Scholars laid the cobbles in front of the school with stones collected from the River Dove in 1607, for which they were given 18 pennies in bread, cheese and drink for their work. The school and associated masters' houses are now private dwellings. (8)

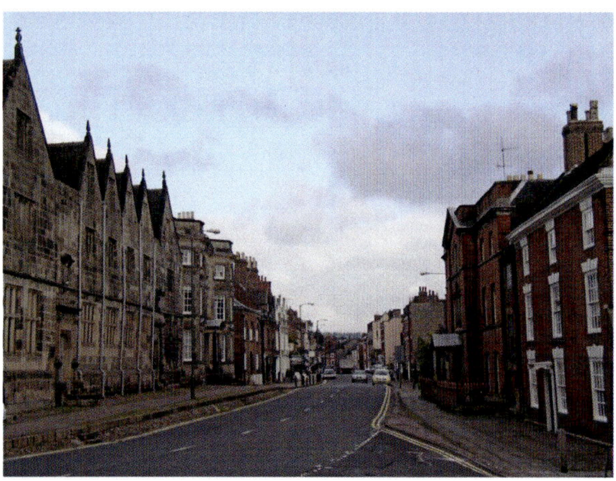

The next building is ***The Grey House***, with the best Georgian frontage in Ashbourne. This house was originally built around 1750 for Francis Higginbotham, a local lawyer. Unfortunately, he was not able to enjoy his new home for long as he appears to have been forced to leave Ashbourne having incurred the displeasure of the local squire, Leak Okeover, for marrying his sister. The house was then sold to Brian Hodgson, a businessman with inns at Buxton and Stamford and considerable investments in copper mining. Despite the fact that the house was only a few years old, Hodgson commissioned the Derby architect, Joseph Pickford, to add a new stone front in line with the latest architectural developments, which Pickford possibly learnt whilst working for Robert Adam at Kedleston Hall.

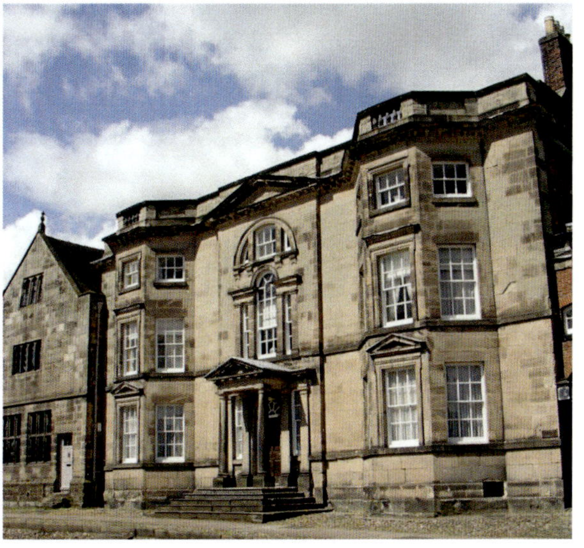

The red brick building to the right of The Grey House was its former ***coach house and stables.*** The right of the building was for the coachman, whilst the left side was for the coach; the arched bay had two large wooden doors to receive coach shafts. The building was converted into two houses in 1927.

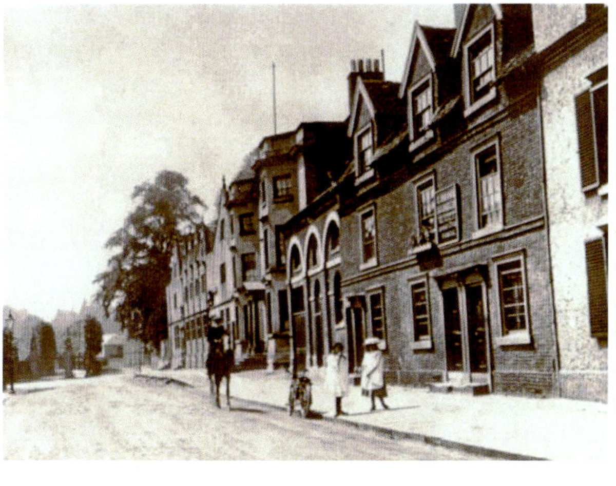

Continue back towards the town centre to reach The Ivies (No 49), a large house with the door approached by steps and a basement.

The next major building is ***The Ivies***, built around 1785 by the Dale family who had invested in local cotton spinning mills. It has the appearance of a London town house. Look for the bell pull and speaking tube on either side of the door, and at the front door itself: does the saltire cross on the door (unusual in Ashbourne) indicate that the builder was a supporter of Bonnie Prince Charlie? (who we will meet again later in the tour). At the side of The Ivies a yard leads to a former coach house.

Cross over the former railway bridge

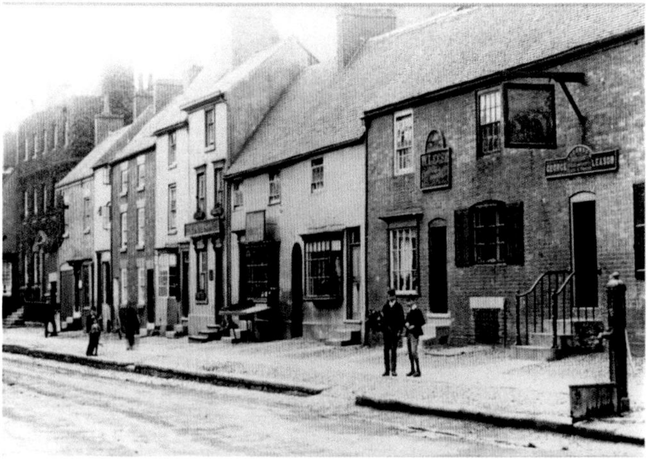

The extension of the railway line from Ashbourne to Buxton in 1899 resulted in the demolition of a row of houses to create a bridge and tunnel entrance. The railway was never profitable and Regular passenger services ended in 1954; the line continued to be used for freight, excursions and winter emergencies until its final closure in 1964. But it left a good legacy, as the route is now the ***Tissington Trail*** for walkers and cyclists. Since the tunnel was re-opened in 2000, the trail runs into the town centre, and it now attracts more users than passengers who travelled on the trains.

By the side of the bridge is the timber-framed building that was the ***Old Bear Inn***, now Spurrier Smith Antiques. The inn catered mainly for the inhabitants of the nearby yards and was one of the inns used to house French prisoners of war in Napoleonic times. Between 1802 and 1814 a total of 172 French prisoners were housed in Ashbourne, with about 40 at any given time. They were required to stay within one mile of the town and to observe a curfew. Ten married local girls, but neither the British nor the French Governments approved of these weddings.

Immediately after the antiques shop turn left and walk through the tunnel entrance to the Yard.

Smith's Yard climbs the hillside by means of a series of flights of steps. A number of yards survive in Ashbourne and can be explored. They were built on medieval **burgage plots** – narrow strips of land with a building at the front and a long croft (garden) behind. As the population expanded, space between the buildings became sparse and parts of the medieval crofts were built on to form yards containing workshops storerooms and cottages. Yards were usually entered through a 'tunnel' and, in some cases as here, the yard ran through to the narrow back lane at the end of the crofts. The yards leading off the main streets were an important part of the close-knit community in the town centre. In 1851, there were about twenty-five yards housing around 750 people, about a quarter of the town's population. Most yards had a public house at the entrance. This yard housed higher status families than most of the other yards in Ashbourne. It now has a garden on the west side of the yard, but this was once the site of a brass foundry and local clock manufacturer. (9)

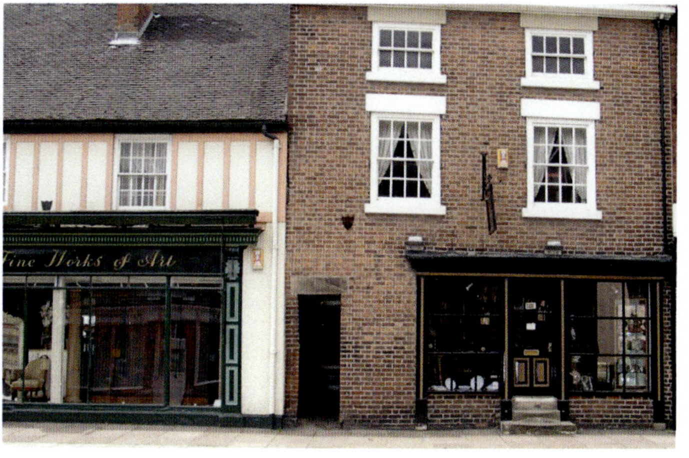

In Victorian times, there were six family firms of clockmakers in Ashbourne. There are still three today; one, Haycocks in North Lees, had an earlier workshop in ***Smith's Yard.***

Return back down Smith's Yard and turn left to reach a stone fronted building (31 Church Street)

This building, now a private house, was the ***Trustee Savings Bank*** with a stone frontage from 1834. The wording of Trustee Savings Bank can just be seen above the western doorway. In Victorian times, the room on the first floor was used as a school by the bank's actuary and a later actuary was the editor of the Ashbourne News Telegraph – obviously not a full-time job!

Continue to Hamilton House (27 Church Street)

Hamilton House is one of the few properties in Ashbourne with Regency features, including a fine fanlight and cast iron balcony. It was the Victorian home of **Louis Bosworth Hurt**, who was popular for his paintings of Highland cattle. Recently, one of his paintings sold at auction for £78,000. Later it was the home of ***Foster's Fishing Tackle***, a major industry in the town where Foster was known as the *"Amiable Angler of the Dove"*.

Continue to Manion Antiques

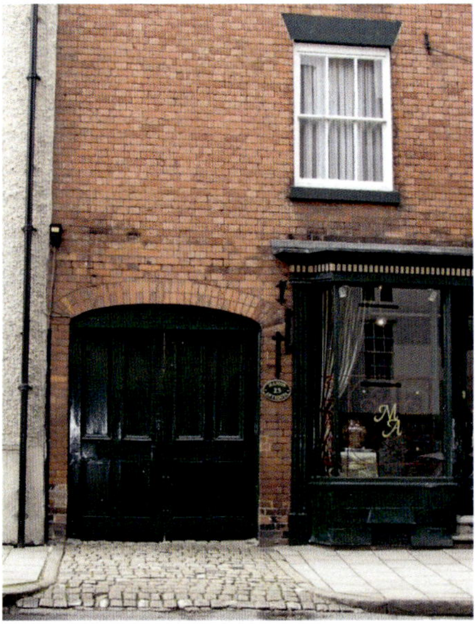

Nos. 21-23 Church Street were part of a late Georgian commercial property, to which a later double shop front was added in the middle of the 19th century. At the rear of the shop, behind the closed carriage doors there is a Grade II listed derelict malthouse of 1785. At one time, there were seven malthouses in Ashbourne. This was also the site of a rope-walk for rope manufacture and leather tanning. The combination of the smells from the production of malt (pleasant) and the tanning of leather (unpleasant, as urine and dung were used in the process) would have made the house an interesting place to live in Georgian times.

Continue to Vine House (15 Church Street)

Vine House is a brick house of around 1740 built on a stone basement with a Tudor mullioned window from an earlier house. An iron palisade, with a vine growing behind flanks the imposing entrance with its columns. John Alsop, a lawyer and local landowner lived here. He was famed for his hard drinking and his love of cockfighting. When asked what time he went to bed he replied, "I don't know, about the time I get drunk, I think!" Squire Alsop achieved a degree of notoriety by nearly causing the death of Dr Johnson by egging him on to eat more and more food at a dinner, until they had to send for a surgeon.

Walk along to Ashbourne Heritage Centre (13 Church Street)

In the 18th century this was the home of Langford family, builders responsible for much development in the town. The site of a pharmacy in Victorian times, a large number of items associated with this trade have been found in the garden. The Heritage Centre also holds many exhibits associated with the history of the town, and a visit is well worthwhile. (10)

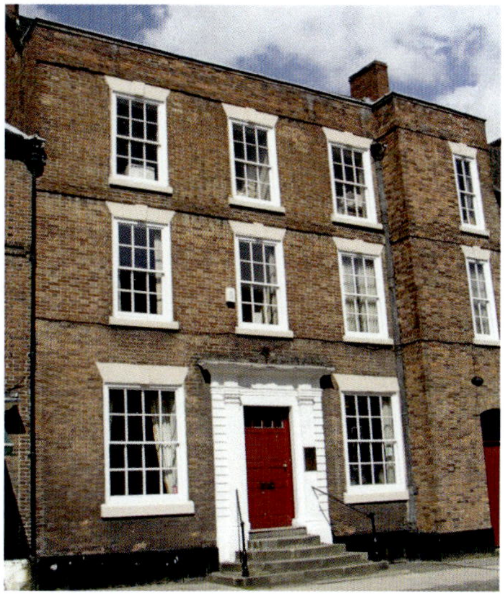

Continue to the dental surgery at Oswald House (7 Church Street)

Another fine gentleman's house of around 1740, ***Oswald House*** has an entrance approached by steps with railings. The two ladies who lived here used to entertain Dr Samuel Johnson to strawberries and tea in their summerhouse which still stands today.

Walk along to the former NatWest Bank opposite Dig Street

This was an important coaching inn, initially the ***Black Greyhound*** and later the ***Wheatsheaf***, and was famous for its strong beer, locally known as " tear brain". When an inn, it had a central carriage entrance that is not visible today.

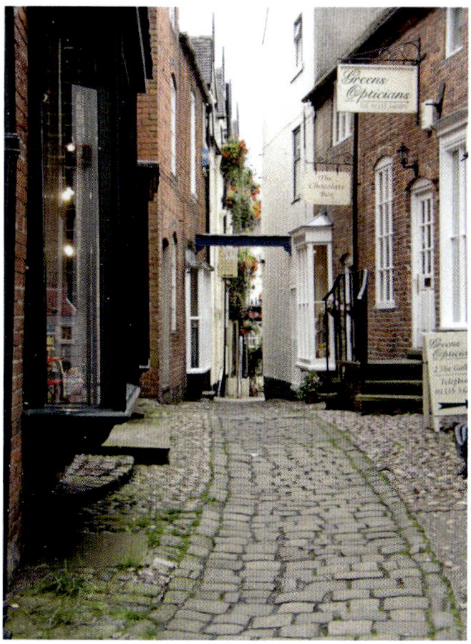

Walk to the bottom of Victoria Square

This was once the start of a large triangular market place, a sign of medieval town planning. It is likely that sometime in the middle of the 13th century, probably after a disastrous fire in 1252, a new town was laid out moving the town centre from around the parish church to its present location. Infill buildings have since divided the market place into three areas: Victoria Square, the Market Place and St John Street. The original buildings would have been two storey timber-frame buildings. As Ashbourne became more prosperous in Georgian times, most around the Market Place were rebuilt as three storeys in brick, although some timber-frame buildings survived; others just had a brick front put onto the original house. You will see examples of these as you continue your walk. In Victorian times, there were 23 public houses in this part of town; today there are just five. Before ascending Victoria Square, look across the road at the ***Green Man Royal Hotel*** and its gallows sign. The Green Man was built in the 1750s to service the growing coaching trade in Ashbourne, and was the town's premier coaching inn. As the coaching trade in Ashbourne reduced in the 1820s, the owner of the Green Man bought the neighbouring Blackamoor's Head and amalgamated the two inns into the Green Man and Black's Head Hotel. In the 1830s, Princess (later Queen) Victoria stopped here for a comfort break on her tour around Britain. A later owner changed the name to The Green Man and Black's Head Royal Hotel. The railways brought a final end to the lucrative coaching trade, but the Green Man continued to be a centre of social activities in Ashbourne until its closure as an inn in 2012. It is now being redeveloped as a complex of shops and offices, as well as a café, pub and hotel rooms. The **gallows sign** across the street is one of the few left in Britain. The head on top of the sign is smiling as you enter town and frowning as you leave. (11)

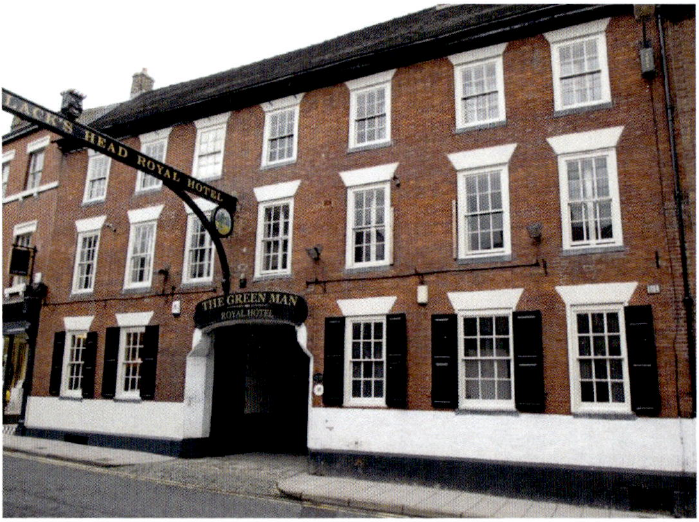

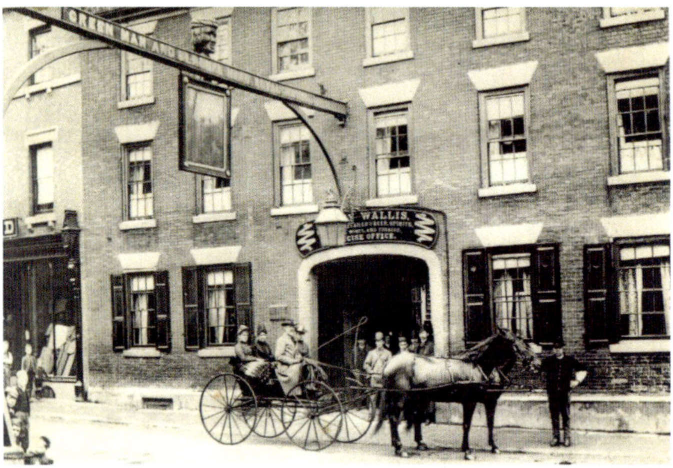

Local legend holds that Sir Walter Raleigh owned property in the town, and he had a black servant boy who became somewhat of a celebrity when his master was visiting Ashbourne. He was known for his broad smile but, as he was reluctant to leave, he had a frown on his face as he looked back.

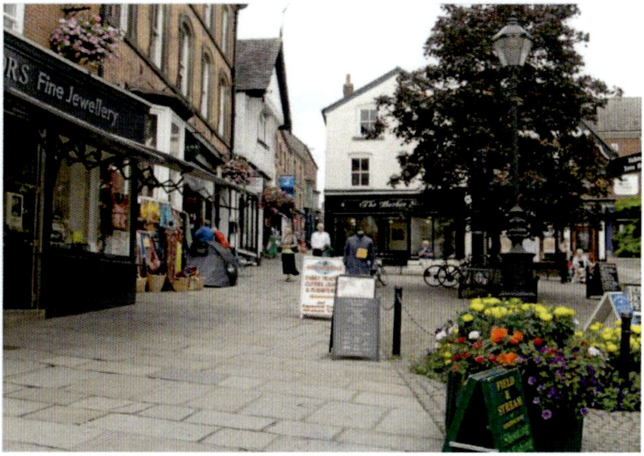

Victoria Square was originally known as The Butchery, as it was the site of the town's butcher shops; the meat would have been displayed on wooden boards or 'shambles' Spot the **mounting block in front of *The Flower Shop*.** Such blocks were used to help people get into carriages or mount horses. Also look above the **bookmakers**, to the right of the Leek Building Society, where you can see one of the few **sundials** left in Ashbourne. If the sun is shining, check its accuracy. The **lamp post** was originally erected at the bottom of the Market Place when gas lighting was introduced into the town in the 1840s. It was moved when the road was widened and now, powered by electricity, is a memorial to the group of businessmen who founded the Ashbourne Gas Company.

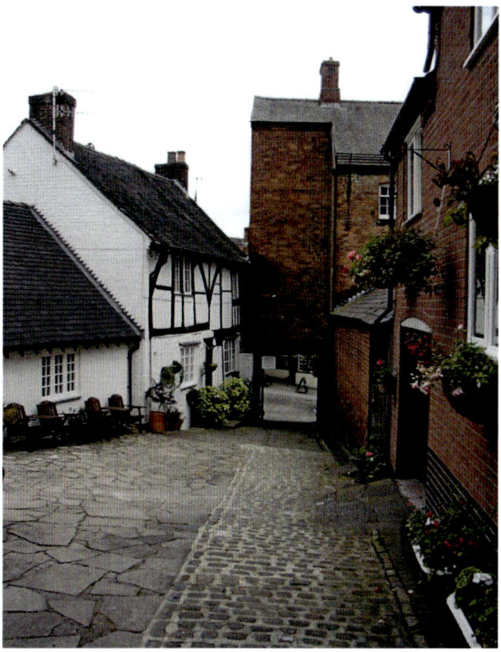

Walk to the entry by the Lamplight Restaurant, and enter Tiger Yard

This is the ***Tiger Yard***, a good example of an Ashbourne yard. This one was named after the Tiger Inn, now the Lamplight Restaurant, at its entrance. (12) The cobbles and stone sets in the ***Lamplight Restaurant.*** This is one of the surviving timber-frame buildings in the town. It is a good example of how buildings were 'modernised' to keep up with building fashions. In Tiger Yard, you can see the Tudor timber and brick construction; recently some timbers were dated to 1493. In Georgian times, a brick front was added whilst, in the Victorian period, the front was rendered and decorative bargeboards were installed. Finally, in the 20th century, a large glass window was added for an Italian restaurant.

Return to Victoria Square, turn left and enter the next yard, Peach's Butcher.

This is ***Shakespeare's Yard,*** named after a butcher who owned the shop by the entrance in the 19th century. He was an accomplished musician and poet, who claimed that he inherited his abilities from the Bard. There was a slaughterhouse behind the shop and its surface drain can still be seen in the yard. After the cattle market was moved in the late 19th century, cattle were herded down this lane to a slaughter-house.

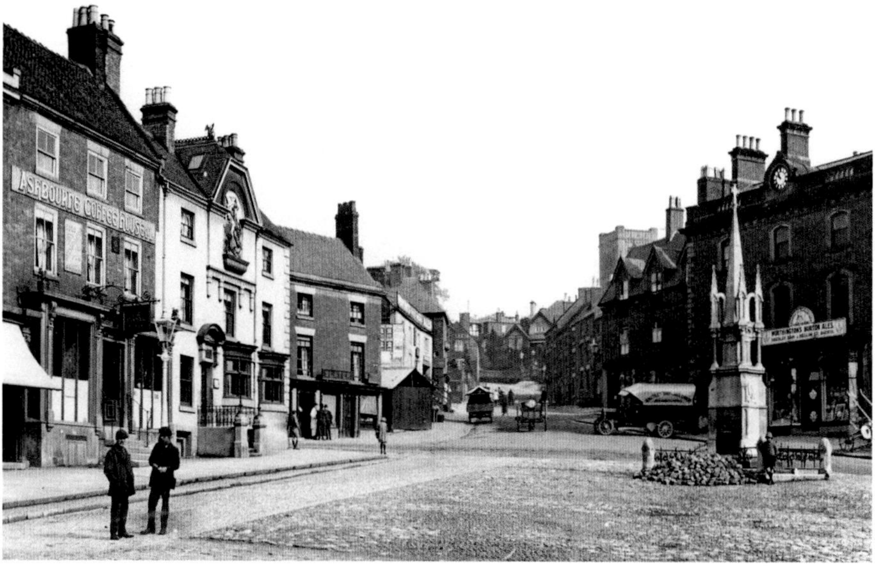

Return to Victoria Square and walk uphill into the Market Place

Traditionally pigs were sold at the top of the Market Place in the pig market (now Buxton Road) sheep in Mutton Lane (now King Street), chickens in the Poultry (now Union Street), wheat in front of the ***George and Dragon*** and horses and cattle at the bottom of the hill.

Take some time to look at the rooflines of the buildings, which give an indication of the original size of the buildings. When the market was built all properties were the same width but many have now been linked together. This can be seen clearly with the two adjacent buildings now occupied by ***Fat Face*** and formerly Spencer's Bakery.

Walk to the Wright Memorial at the top of the Market Place

The location of a medieval market was marked by a cross, which helped to remind traders to be honest as God was watching their transactions. However, Ashbourne's market cross was further down the hill and the ***Wright Memorial*** is a Victorian addition. It was *"Erected by public subscription to the memory of Francis Wright as a record of his valuable services to this town and neighbourhood".* **(13)**

Wright came from a Nottingham banking family, which had married into the local gentry, he was a successful businessman, entrepreneur, and benefactor. He was also the principal shareholder and a director of The Butterley Company, which, amongst other things, provided the bricks and ironwork for St Pancras Station in London.

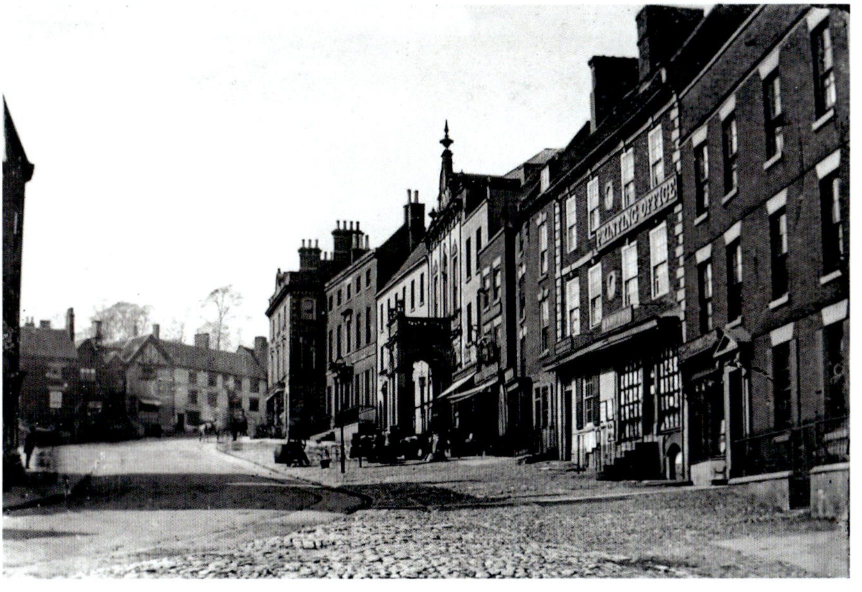

Wright believed '*busy hands kept the devil away*'. As Chairman of the Magistrates, he tried to impose his moral principles on the town. He put a stop to the town's annual fairs and tried to stop the Shrovetide Football.

The game always used to start in the Market Place until Wright's opposition forced a move onto Shaw Croft, then private land, and the magistrates could not prevent the game starting there, as it still does to this day. Now it is a public car park and has to be cleared of cars for the two days of the game. Because of his opposition to Shrovetide, he was known locally as the *"President of the Poke-your-nose-into-every-body's-business Society".*

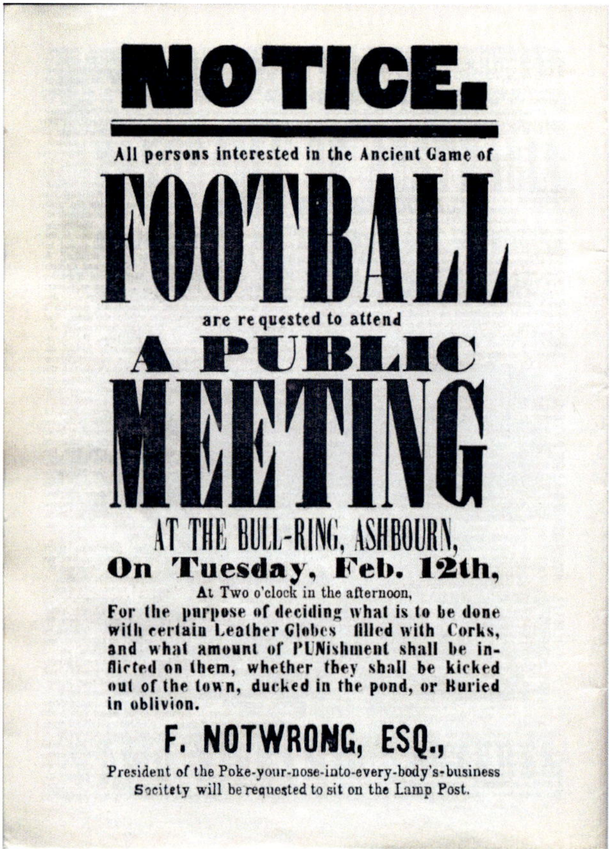

NOTICE.

All persons interested in the Ancient Game of

FOOTBALL

are requested to attend

A PUBLIC MEETING

AT THE BULL-RING, ASHBOURN,

On Tuesday, Feb. 12th,

At Two o'clock in the afternoon,

For the purpose of deciding what is to be done with certain Leather Globes filled with Corks, and what amount of PUNishment shall be inflicted on them, whether they shall be kicked out of the town, ducked in the pond, or Buried in oblivion.

F. NOTWRONG, ESQ.,

President of the Poke-your-nose-into-every-body's-business Socitety will be requested to sit on the Lamp Post.

Perhaps he was not as popular locally as the Memorial suggested. After falling out with the vicar of St Oswald's Parish Church, he built ***St John's Church*** in 1872; its tower can be seen if you step back and look up Buxton Road hill. There is an extension to this tour to St John's Church if time permits.

The town's **bullring** was nearby and, it was here in 1745, that the Young Pretender, **Bonnie Prince Charlie**, declared his father to be King James III. He stayed at Ashbourne Hall and his troops camped in the hall grounds (now the town park) before marching onto Derby. After three days there, his generals persuaded him that they would not be successful and he reluctantly agreed to return to Scotland. The retreating army looted on their return and the landlord of the Royal Oak, an inn at Hanging Bridge over the Dove which still exists today, was shot for refusing to hand over his horse.

If you look down the Market Place, the ***fish and chip shop*** is one of the original timber-frame buildings, possibly the oldest in town as it was recently dated to 1420. In the past it was the Brown Lion public house. Look across the street at the houses opposite and you can see how some have been joined together. ***The Salvation Army shop*** is a combination of a two and three storey house.

Cross the road at the pedestrian crossing

Immediately in front of you is the ***Town Hall*** (more properly ***the Market Hall***). This is one of the few Victorian buildings in the Market Place. It is faced with ashlar stone in an Italianate style. The stone pediment at the top of the building shows the date 1861 along with the names of the trustees. It was built on the site of the Talbot Inn, mentioned by Izaak Walton and Charles Cotton's *The Compleat Angler.* In the book, 'Piscator' (fisherman) and Viator' (traveler) 'stop for a drink at the Talbot. When asked if he wants ale or wine, Viator replied, *"I am for Country liquor, Derbyshire ale if you please; for a Man should not me-thinks come from London to drink wine in the Peak".* The building continues to be used for entertainment and special markets, and the town's council chamber is at the rear of the building. There is a commemorative plaque to Bonnie Prince Charlie's visit on the front of the Town Hall. (14)

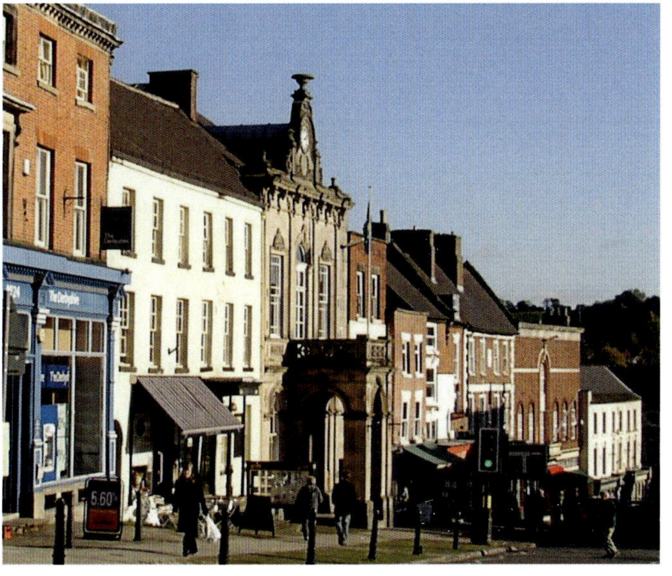

Walk between the two milestones on either side of the Town Hall entrance

You will see that you have covered eight miles, as one milestone gives the distance to London as 'miles 139', whilst the other states it is 147. The one on the left of the entrance is Georgian and was erected during the coaching era, when six coaching routes passed through the town and refers to the distance to Charing Cross in London (139 miles). The other milestone is modern and is one of 11 in Derbyshire that commemorate the passage of the Olympic torch through Derbyshire in 2012. The distance is to the Olympic Stadium in east London (147 miles). The poem on top relates to the Registry Office which was located in the Town Hall when the stone was erected.

Walk through the tunnel entrance to the right of the Town Hall.

This is ***Town Hall Yard*** and is a typical mid-Victorian development of workers' cottages. Just above the entrance to the Yard is small brass memorial to **Mr Tom Fearn**, aged 40, who was killed when the balance bar fell from the fire bell, which used to be situated above this entrance, and was being rung because of a report of a fire. The bell was used to alert the fire crews to man the fire engine, which was kept at the rear of the George and Dragon. Sadly, on this tragic occasion, the alert proved to be a false alarm. Some of Mr Fearn's descendants still live in the town, and arranged for this monument to be erected in his honour.

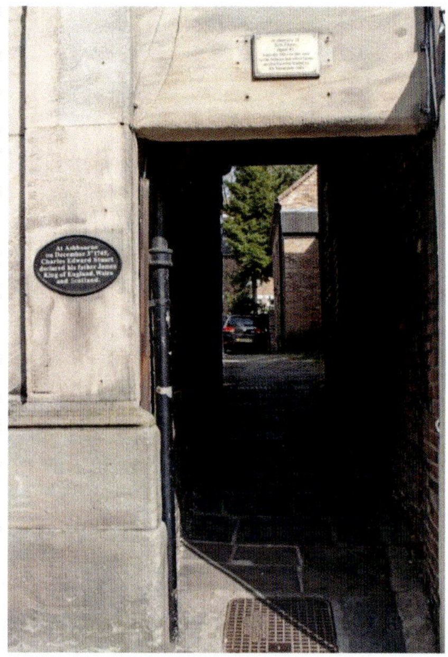

Head up the hill to a set of steps with date 1712 above

Here in 1772, ***John Wesley*** preached to a large crowd. After preaching in Derby Market Place, Wesley arrived in Ashbourne at 9am, but found the house where he intended to preach "*would not hold a quarter of the people*", and so his service was delivered in the open air. Wesley commented that "*none offered the least rudeness*". This was not always the case in some towns.

(THE ST JOHN'S CHURCH EXTENSION STARTS HERE: see Extension No 1)

If you are not doing the extension to St John's Church retrace your steps down the hill.

The building next to the steps is ***Monument House***, once the home of George Brittlebank, a local solicitor. He was a keen supporter of the Shrovetide Football game and an opponent of Francis Wright. When Wright tried to stop the game, Brittlebank called out as the ball was 'turned up' (thrown to start the game): *"play up lads, play up and if you are charged, I will defend you for nothing"*. He was the first to be arrested and fined 40shillings (£2).!

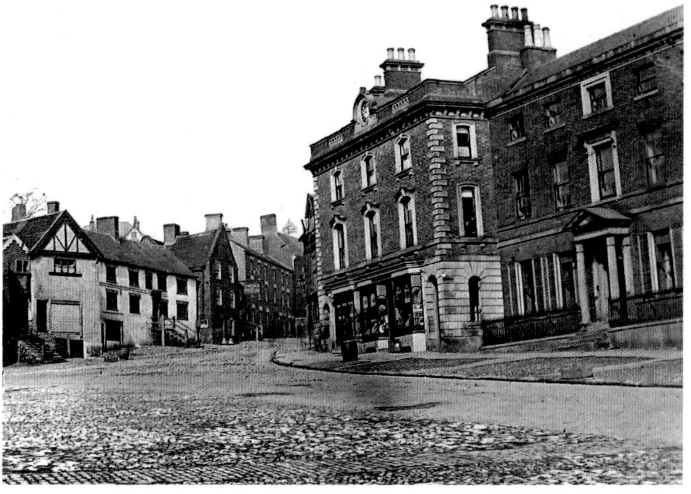

Look into the ***Silvarious*** shop where you can see the timber framework, uncovered by the owner during some recent renovations. The front of the building, which features some lintels at alarming angles, is a later addition.

Walk down the hill

Pass the two **red phone boxes**, which are listed buildings in their own right. The building now used by the ***Nottingham Building Society*** was built around 1690 and is believed to be the oldest brick building in the Market Place. Next door was built as the ***Elite Cinema*** in the 1930s but, surprisingly, does not look out of place next to a building 240 years older. Look down the hill at ***Smith's Tavern***; this narrow building occupies a remnant of a medieval burgage plot.

Cross the road carefully at the traffic island

Look at the entrance alongside ***Ryman***. This is ***Prince's Gate*** where, in 1928**, HRH The Prince of Wales** walked through to 'turn up' the ball for the Shrovetide Football game. A temporary wooded structure was built behind here so the Prince could throw the ball into Shawcroft. Compare the spelling on the two memorials above the entrance. (Should it be Prince's or Princess Gate?)

Walk along St John Street towards the gallows sign

This street was probably named after the Knights of St John, who had a hospital in Ashbourne. ***The Gingerbread Cafe*** on your left is one of the buildings in the town that dates from the Tudor period. People have shopped here for 500 years. When the shop was built around 1492, it was three separate units. Inside the café area, some lath and plaster has been exposed for all to see. The neighbouring ***Natural Choice*** is also timber-framed behind the somewhat bland brick front; inside you can see its cruck frame construction, recently dated to 1526. During Victorian times, the shop was a druggist and grocer. After spells as an electrical goods shop and a record store, its use came full circle when, in 1991, Steve and Roy Parker moved their health food business into it. (15)

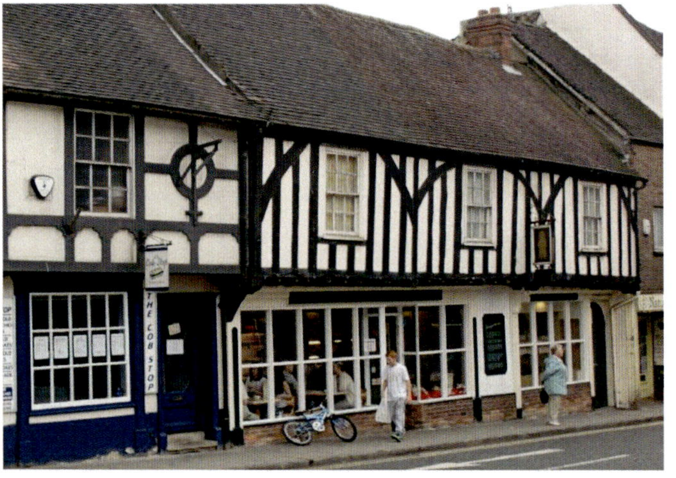

Walk to the passageway between the greengrocers and the shoe shop.

The shop in front of you is ***Wigley's,*** selling and originally making shoes since the 1830s. It was once part of the ***Blackamoor's Head Inn*** - another

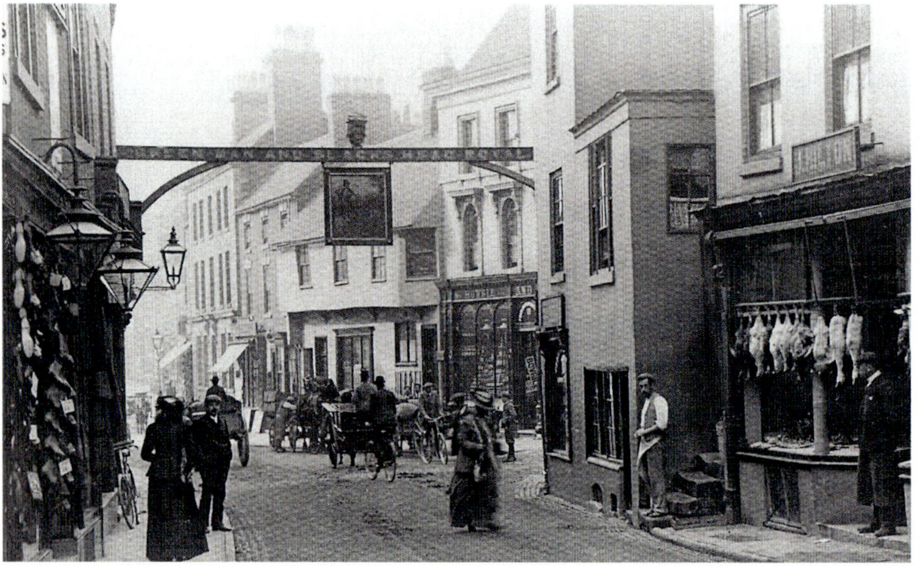

of the coaching inns in Ashbourne until purchased by the owner of the Green Man. The town lacked a purpose-built assembly room and the Blackamoor's Head was the venue for most of the town's social activities until it closed. Assemblies were an essential feature of Georgian life and were held regularly throughout the year.

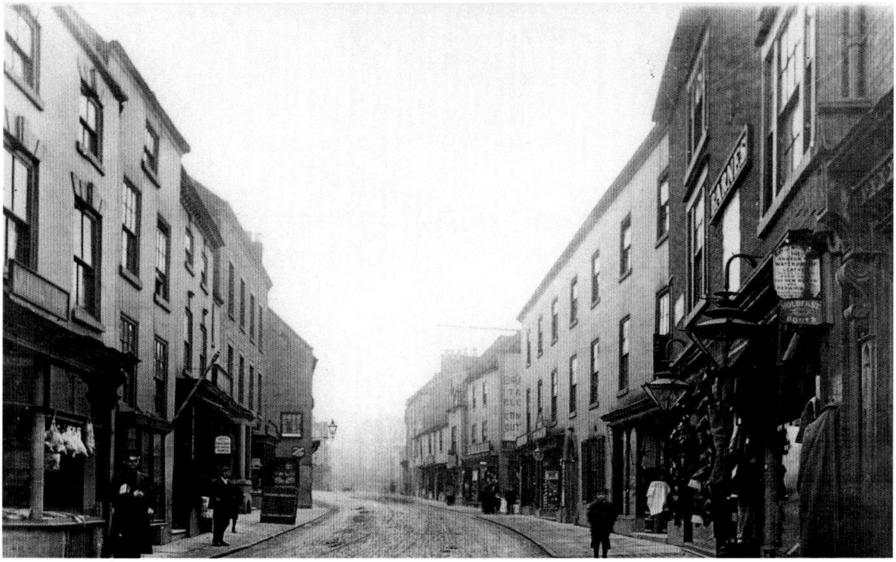

A writer described such assemblies as *"the resort of the young and gay, who go to see and be seen; and also of those who, having played their matrimonial cards well in earlier life, are now content to sit down to a sober game of whist*". Not everyone visiting the inn would have been in a good mood, though, as its assembly rooms were also used for the local magistrate and county courts.

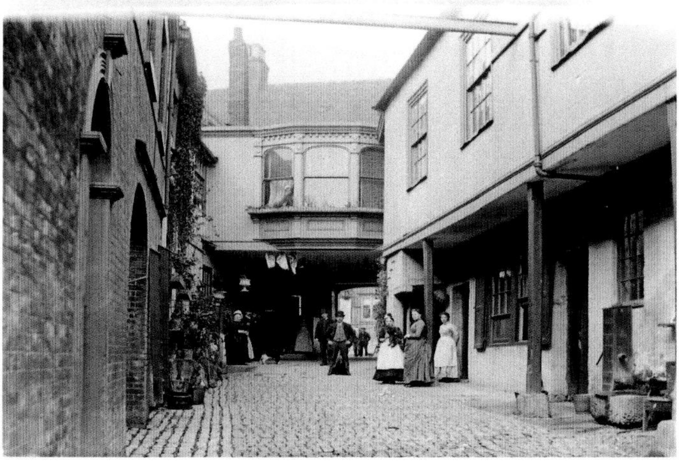

Walk down Horse and Jockey Yard to Shaw-croft car park

Horse and Jockey Yard is named after a public house that stood on the other side of the entrance to the Blackamoor's Head. Walk down to ***Shawcroft*** car park, which is the starting place for the annual **Shrovetide Football game.** The game starts at the **turn-up plinth** by the vehicle entrance to the car park. It is played throughout the streets, alleyways, in the park pond and across fields with three miles separating the goals: Sturston Mill for the Up'ards and Clifton Mill for the Down'ards. Traditionally goals were scored by tapping the ball against the mill wheel. Since both mills are now demolished, purpose-built stone plinths were erected as the goals on the riverbank. Not quite as lawless as its reputation, the game has only a few rules and play is not allowed in gardens, the churchyard or the Memorial Gardens, but most shops still board up their windows. Although mainly a game of 'hug' where the ball is carried around in a large group of players, the ball is quite often in the air where spectators can see it, and there are occasional breakaways. One of the most popular origin theories is that the game started in Saxon times when the ball was the severed head of a defeated enemy, which was tossed into the waiting crowd, but there is no real evidence supporting this theory.

(THE PARK AND ASHBOURNE HALL EXTENSION STARTS HERE: see Extension No 2)

If you are not doing this extension, walk past the public toilets to the pedestrian exit from the car park alongside Waitrose to return to the library.

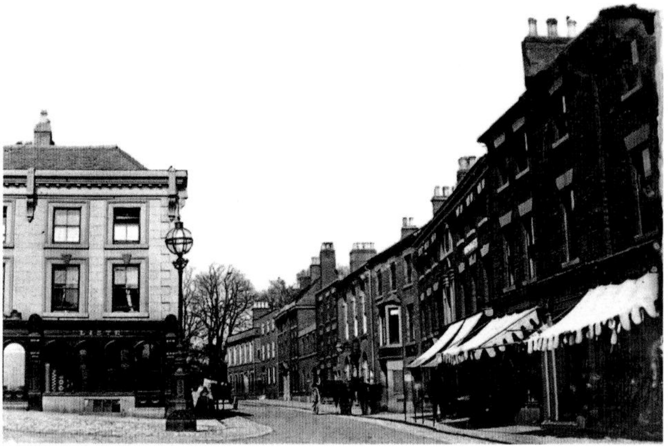

WALK EXTENSION 1: TO ST JOHN'S CHURCH

Continue up the hill, crossing King Street carefully and look at the houses on both sides of the road.

The properties on this side of the road, a row of stepped brick terraced houses, date from the early 19th century. The other side of the road is more varied. The oldest building **No. 4 (*Whites*)** - which was the White Lion pub - is a two storey property from the late 17th century. Below it, **No. 2** is an early 19th century, three storey building with a late 19th century shop front. **Nos. 6-10** (also part of Whites) are a large three storey Victorian building with original stables behind. Above this are a pair of fine double-fronted houses (**Nos.**

12 & 14) built in the late 18th century and almost intact with multi-paned windows, painted timber doorcases with triangular pediments, decorative brick eaves, stone-capped roof gables and large central brick chimney stacks.

Walk up to the church gates and enter the churchyard

St John's Church was built in 1871 at a cost of £8,000 to accommodate a congregation who had split off from St Oswald's Church. Its benefactor, Francis Wright of Osmaston Manor, is thought to have had a disagreement with the clergy of St Oswald's parish church. Wright was a low-churchman, who disapproved of the vicar's high church leanings and his desire to end the private ownership of pews.

St John's originally opened as a 'free' church with a board of trustees formed by Francis Wright. However, after Wright's death, the church ran into financial difficulties and eventually joined the Church of England in 1883 as a 'peculiar' - a church without a parish. The church is now governed by the board of trustees and sits within the parish of Ashbourne.

Henry Isaac Stevens of Derby built the church in a variation of the Romanesque style. Stevens was involved in work on many Derbyshire churches including nearby Osmaston and Fenny Bentley. Over the door you will see the words from Matthew 18:20: *"Where two or three are gathered together in my name, there I am in the midst of them"* indicating a gathering of the faithful as opposed to Wright's opinion of the parish church congregation.

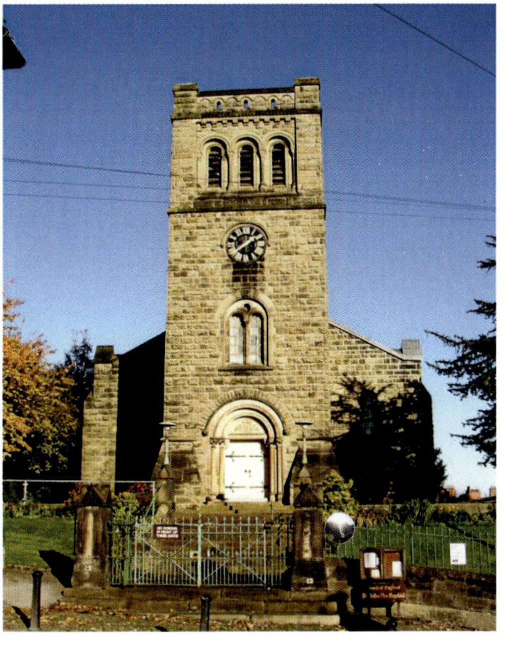

When you enter the church you will see that it has a spacious open interior with tall slim iron columns and narrow aisles. The intention was probably to create a large open worship area with excellent acoustics, with the pulpit, where the gospel is preached, as the most important item. The gallery would have been intended for singers, in contrast to the location of the choir in the chancel of the parish church. Inside St John's, there is a 'gothic' memorial to Francis Wright, who was not able to enjoy his church for long as he died only two years after its completion. The **east window,** a WW1 memorial, is a fine example of the work of AJ Davies from the Birmingham School of Art - one of the leading centres for the Arts and Crafts movement.

The fine acoustics and large seating capacity mean that the church is often used during the Ashbourne Festival for concerts and lectures.

Return back down the hill to the Market Place

WALK EXTENSION 2: ASHBOURNE HALL AND TOWN PARK

Walk across Shawcroft car park to the turn-up steps by the entrance

This is where Shrovetide Football is started by 'turning up' the ball from the plinth by throwing it into the 'hug' of the players. Up until 1891, the Down'ards captain started the game on Shrove Tuesday, and the Up'ards on Ash Wednesday. Since 1891, a local dignitary or occasionally a celebrity has been invited to perform the honour. Twice the ball has been turned up by a Prince of Wales; in 1928 by the later Edward VIII and in 2003 by Prince Charles. On one side of the plinth are the words of the Shrovetide Anthem sung at the pre-game lunch. The car park is cleared of cars for the two days of play. (17)

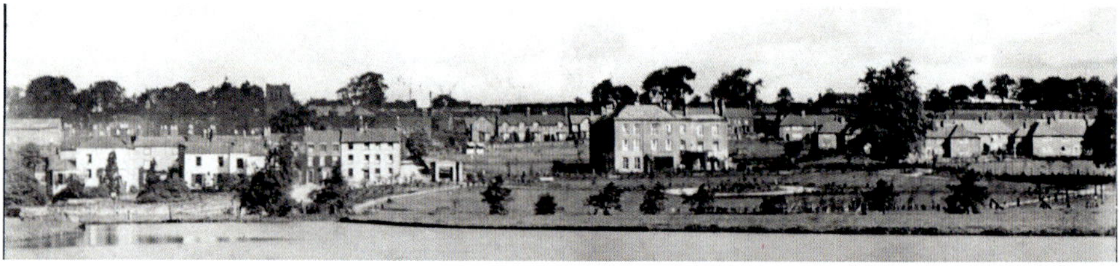

Cross the road at the pedestrian crossing and enter the park via the ramp over the town's flood defence wall

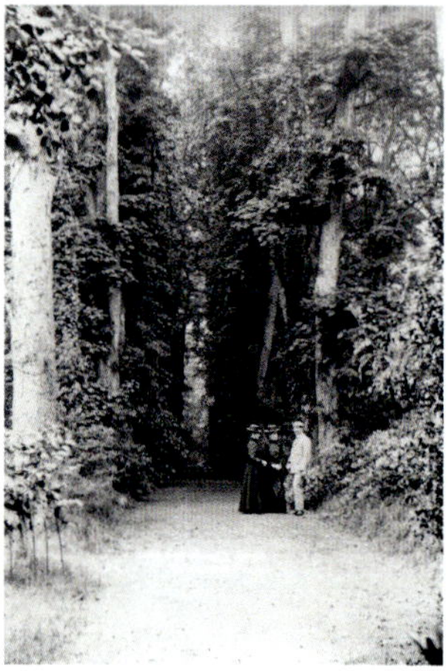

Ashbourne Park became part of the Ashbourne Hall estate sometime after 1150, and was used for hunting deer. It was developed into a 'pleasure garden' by the Boothby family from the late 17th century, and was further enlarged by Brooke Boothby in 1785 when he rebuilt Ashbourne Hall. Many trees were planted and the fishponds were reshaped into ornamental lakes. In 1922, the estate was sold off with much of the ornamental gardens becoming municipal housing. The remainder of the estate became the ***Memorial Gardens*** **and** ***Recreation Ground.*** The ***War Memorial Gates,*** by Lomas and Sons of Derby were unveiled in 1922 by Lord Cullen of Ashbourne and are the site of the annual service on Remembrance Sunday. (18)

Exit through the small gate to the side to see the front of the memorial

This lists the town's fallen from both world wars. The small additional plaque on the bottom left pillar lists five Ashbourne soldiers who died in WW1, but were not included on the original memorial. After the new plaque was added, the memorial was re-dedicated in May 2012. **(19)**

Return to the park and walk around the gardens to reach a memorial to Catherine Booth

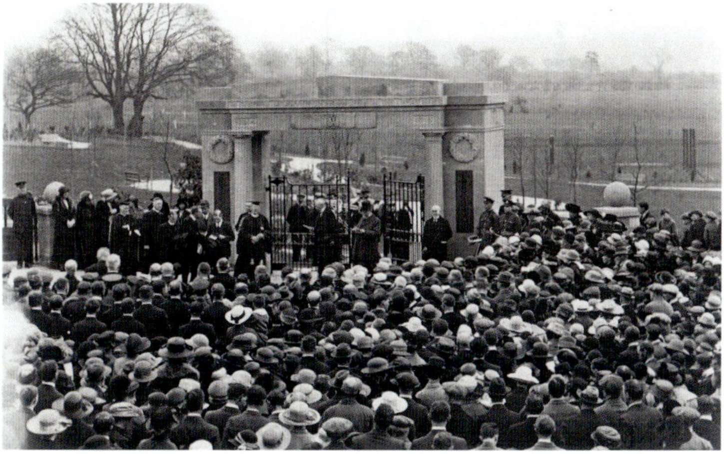

Catherine Booth (née Mumford) was the wife of William Booth, the founder of the Salvation Army. She was born in humble circumstances in Ashbourne on 17 January 1829 at 13 Sturston Road (not included on the walking tour) – this small cottage can still be seen and is marked by a plaque. Her father, John Mumford, was a wheelwright and an itinerant preacher, and the family had moved to Ashbourne in 1827. The major influence on Catherine's life was her mother, Sarah. When they moved to Ashbourne, Sarah started to attend St Oswald's Church but was unhappy there, and as the Methodists gathered strength locally, Sarah became a convert imprinting Methodism on her daughter.

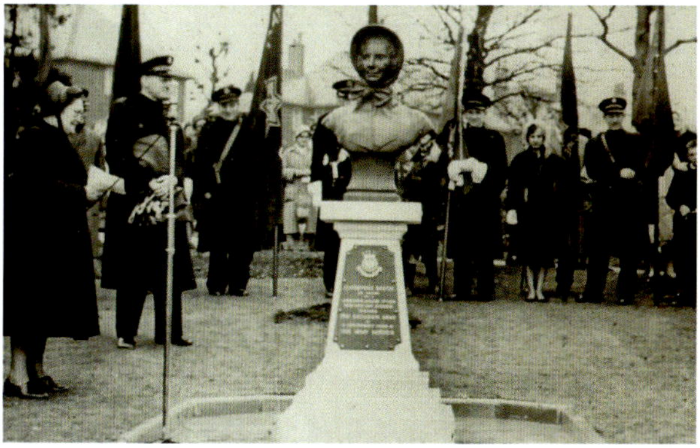

After several family moves Catherine met her future husband William Booth, from Nottingham, in London. They married in 1855 and became itinerant preachers. **(20)**

In 1865, William became involved in East London Christian Mission, whilst Catherine preached in the wealthier parts of London to raise funds. They went on to found the **Salvation Army**, which offered a path to God along with a wide range of welfare initiatives and was the fastest growing religious movement of late Victorian Britain. By the time of Catherine's death in 1890, there were 3,996 centres of work, over 85 social welfare projects and the Army was operating in 32 countries worldwide. The Methodist Times, who called her "the greatest Methodist woman of her generation", recognized her contribution. 50,000 people filed past her coffin at Olympia, west London and the numbers at her funeral had to be limited to 10,000.

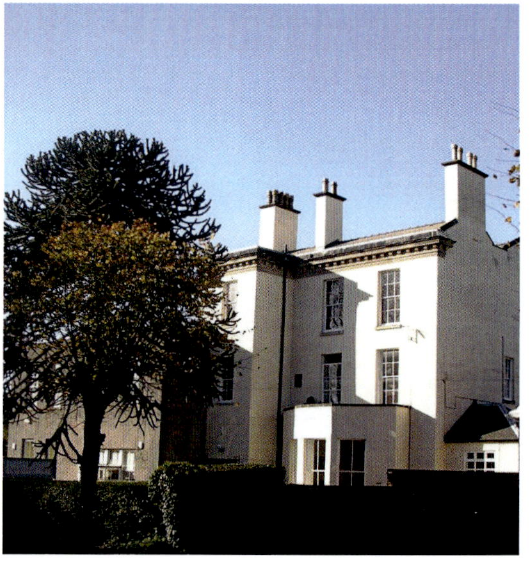

Look across the hedge into the Recreation Ground

In July 1966, the **West German soccer team** practiced during the early rounds of the World Cup before going onto lose to England in the final. The team stayed at the nearby Peveril of the Peak Hotel whilst playing their early matches at Sheffield and Birmingham. This German invasion was well received locally. A different invasion occurred in 1745, when **Bonnie Prince Charlie's troops** camped in the grounds of Ashbourne Hall whilst the Prince and his officers requisitioned the Hall, its owners having - perhaps wisely - "*gone into the hills*".

Leave the park, cross the pedestrian crossing and turn left to reach Ashbourne Hall

This large building is all that is left of the 18th century ***Ashbourne Hall***. There was a large timber-framed hall near here in the Tudor period, but the Boothby family replaced this after they took over the estate in the 17th century. All that survives now is a fragment of the large house built by Brooke Boothby around 1785; part is now used as a Masonic Lodge, a holiday let and the rest occupied by ***Betty's Sewing Box***, a vintage tea room and needlework shop. **(21)**

Turn back towards the town centre, cross Hall Lane carefully and enter St John Street

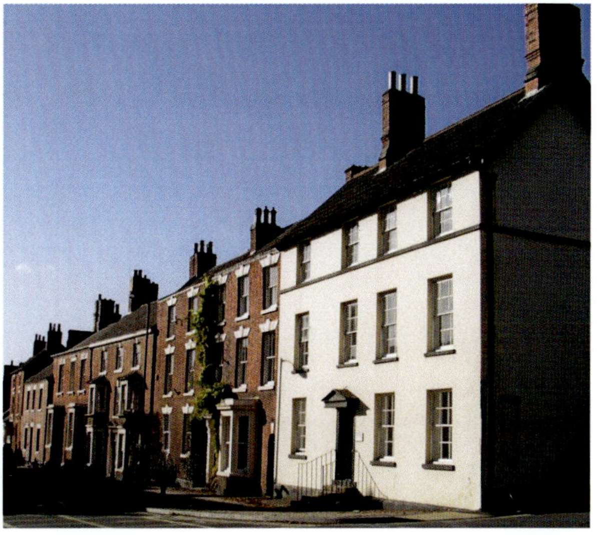

The first house you reach **No. 51 (*Coates & Partners*)** was the residence of the vicar for St John's Church. On the other side of the road is ***Madge House.*** (22) Erasmus Darwin, Charles Darwin's grandfather, bought this property (then the ***Old Nag's Head Inn***) in 1793 for use as a ladies' seminary by his two illegitimate daughters, Susanna and Mary Parker. He paid £700 for the house, an acre of land and a pew in St Oswald's Church for their use. Darwin was critical of the normal education for girls and intended his daughters to put his ideas into practice. He provided the curriculum for the school, including scientific subjects as well as modern languages. He was against stays in a young lady's dress and believed students should be governed by the teacher's mind rather than harsh discipline. He was also a believer in physical education and recommended a diet containing fruit and not too much salt. In many ways he was ahead of his time, and many leading families in the Midlands sent their daughters to the school, although he still advocated that young ladies should be taught *"the charms that enchant all hearts".* The outside of the house, now flats, is little changed from that time. **No. 37** (***Linda Elaine***) is a plain 18th century building with an upstairs room painted with pastoral scenes around 1830, probably by the local artist, Thomas Ravensdale. Next door, **No. 35**, recently had a roof truss dated to 1567. Look across the street at ***St John's House*** with its fine doorway flanked by Tuscan

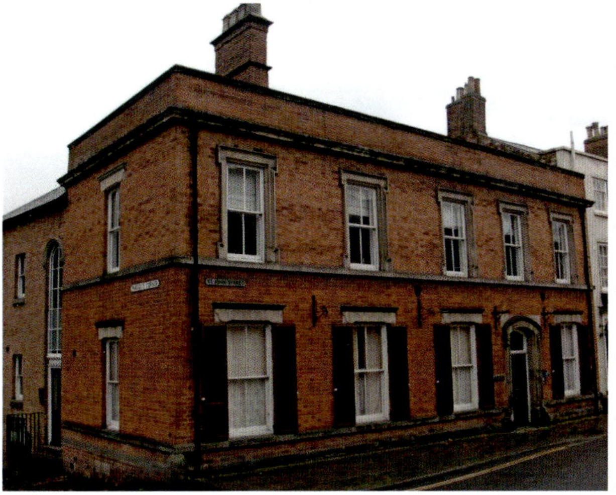

pilasters (a decorative projecting feature) **No. 33 – The Artisan Café Bar and Bottle Shop.** This is another medieval timber-frame building, but its date is unknown as the frame is made from Elm and it is not yet possible to date wood from this tree.

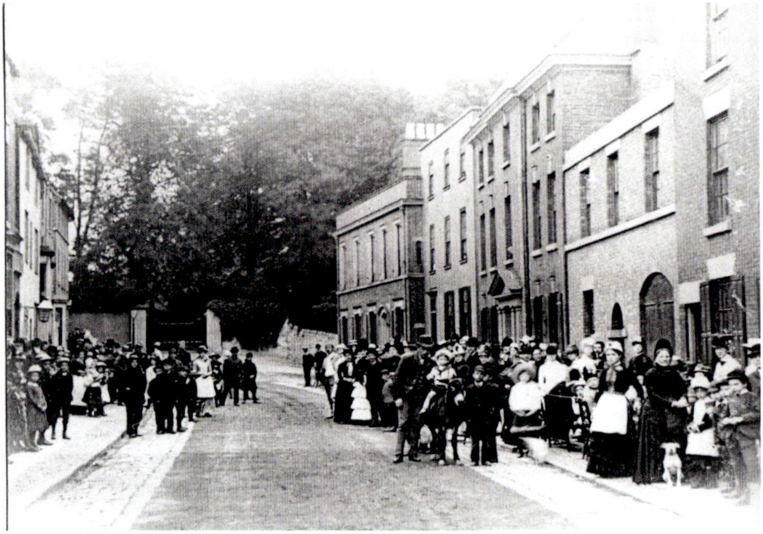

On the other side of the street is **St. John Street Gallery and Café (No 50),** which was built in 1857 as a lecture and meeting hall and leased to Francis Wright as a trustee of the Town's Literary Institute. It provided a place for meetings away from the temptations of alcohol. The County Court moved here in 1861. (16)

Continue along St John Street to the bottom of the Market Place

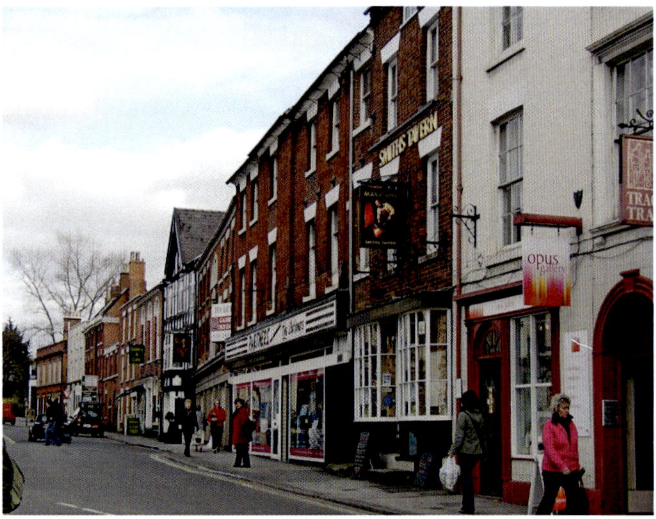

Look across the road at the 2nd and 3rd floor windows in **Nos. 42-44 (the Vision Express building).** These windows are very similar to those used in **The Mansion** and **The Grey House.** However, as this house was built well after Joseph Pickford had died, the work is likely to be by one of his apprentices, possibly using 'stock' auctioned off from his yard at the rear of his house in Friargate, Derby.

Cross the road carefully at the traffic islands and turn left to walk to the yard entrance next to Chimes Café.

This is **Wellington Yard,** named after the neighbouring coaching inn, now the ***Chimes café and clock workshop***; one of the three remaining clock manufacturers in Ashbourne. A surprising number when considering there are only around 30 clock manufacturers in the whole of the country. The mock Tudor frontage and gabled roof were added to the Georgian building in Edwardian times. You can see the old stabling for the inn just before you enter Shawcroft car park.

Walk down the yard to return to Shawcroft car park, and cross to return to the Library.

We hope you have enjoyed your walk around Ashbourne

Index and Guide to the map on the following pages with key places on the trail:

1. Library - *Built in 2012 in Compton - formerly a separate 'township'*
2. Henmore brook - *Traditional boundary between 'Up'ards & Down'ards'*
3. Church Street - *The finest Georgian Street in Derbyshire. (Pevsner)*
4. Clergy Widows Almshouses - *Built in 1770 as '4 neat and tidy houses'*
5. Methodist Chapel - *Distinctive Renaissance-style front by Wills of Derby*
6. The Mansion - *Built around 1680 and regularly visited by Dr Johnson*
7. St Oswald's Church - *Consecrated in 1241 with a 212ft (65m)high spire*
8. Old Grammar School - *Built as a result of the Royal Charter of 1585*
9. Smith's Yard - *A number of hidden yards survive and can be explored.*
10. Heritage Centre - *Holds many interesting items from Ashbournes past.*
11. The Green Man - *A former coaching in with unusual gallows sign.*
12. Tiger Yard - *In Victoria Square, a 15th C timber framed building.*
13. Market Place - *Still the site of a weekly market.*
14. Town Hall - *Built as a Victorian Market Hall in 1861.*
15. Gingerbread Shop - *One of the few original timber framed buildings.*
16. St John's Church - *Built as a result of the 'Pew Wars'*
17. Shrovetide Plinth (turn-up steps) *Where the Shrovetide football starts.*
18. Memorial Gardens and Park - *Part of a medieval hunting 'Park'*
19. Memorial Gates - *A lasting memorial to the fallen of two world wars.*
20. Bust of Catherine Booth - *Mother of the Salvation Army.*
21. Ashbourne Hall - *Remains of the Georgian Hall of 1785.*
22. Madge House - *Home to the two 'natural' daughters of Erasmus Darwin, where they established a girls school using his principles.*

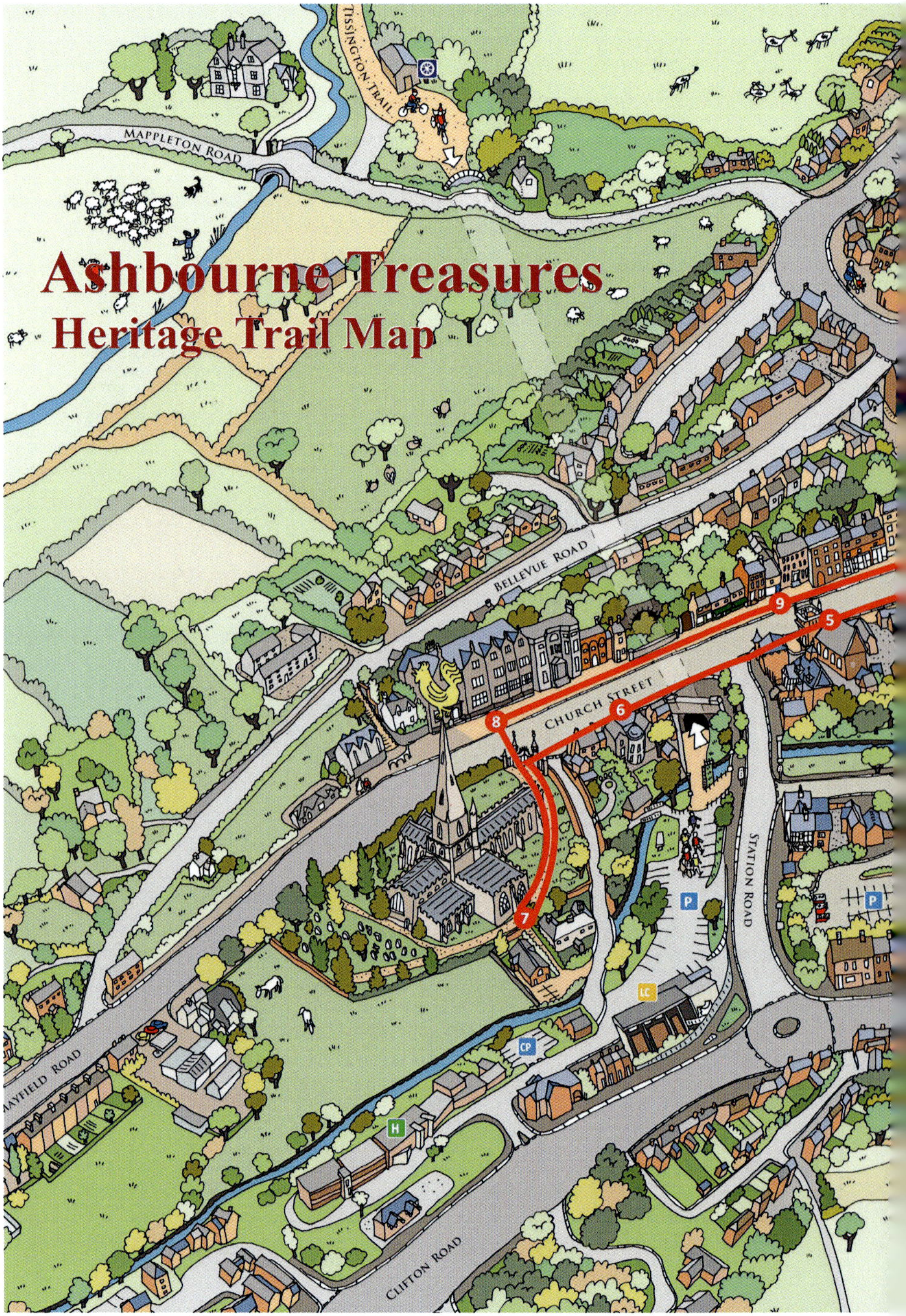

Ashbourne Treasures
Heritage Trail Map
Tissington Trail
Mappleton Road
Bellevue Road
Church Street
Station Road
Mayfield Road
Clifton Road
9
5
8
6
7
P
LC
CP
H